LIVING FOR THE
KINGDOM

TEACHING WHAT JESUS TAUGHT

HAMP LEE III

(com)mission™
PUBLISHING

Living for the Kingdom: Teaching What Jesus Taught/ Hamp Lee III — 1st ed.

ISBN 978-1-940042-20-6

CONTENTS

INTRODUCTION

And Jesus came and spake unto them, saying, All power is given unto me in heaven and in earth. Go ye therefore, and teach all nations, baptizing them in the name of the Father, and of the Son, and of the Holy Ghost: Teaching them to observe all things whatsoever I have commanded you: and, lo, I am with you alway, even unto the end of the world. Amen.[1]

After Jesus had appeared to His 11 disciples, He commissioned them to make disciples of all nations and to teach them to observe everything He commanded them. A disciple is a student of Jesus' teachings. As disciples obey Jesus' commands, they live as lights in the world to reveal the glory of God.[2]

I wrote *Living for the Kingdom: Teaching What Jesus Taught* to fulfill Jesus' Great Commission in Matthew 28:18–20. This book serves as study guide with 115 lessons that outline Jesus' commands throughout the four Gospels.

Making disciples is the greatest mission mankind has ever received. As disciples, we have the honor of serving as Jesus' ambassadors. We display the all-surpassing power and glory of God

---

[1] Matthew 28:18–20.

[2] Matthew 5:14–16; Romans 8:29.

through our lives and good works.[3] With such an important mission, I pray this book will prepare you to fulfill the plan and purpose God has for your life.

---

[3] Matthew 5:14–16; 2 Corinthians 4:7, 5:16–20

STUDENTS
AND TEACHERS

Blessed is the man that walketh not in the counsel of the ungodly, nor standeth in the way of sinners, nor sitteth in the seat of the scornful. But his delight is in the law of the Lord; and in his law doth he meditate day and night. And he shall be like a tree planted by the rivers of water, that bringeth forth his fruit in his season; his leaf also shall not wither; and whatsoever he doeth shall prosper.[4]

Many of us know people who can be considered as ungodly, sinful, and scornful. Some of us talk to them every day. We might think they are smart, funny, and a *little* crazy, but we consider them as good friends and associates. Many of them have been with us through the highest and lowest times of our lives.

Though we hear them share questionable opinions or advice we would never take ourselves, we overlook it. Though we see them do things we would never do, we overlook it. Though we hear them mock others, we laugh along with them and overlook it. Though we would probably tell others to stay away from such people, we have several reasons why we still are with them. Many

---

[4] Psalm 1:1–3.

of us ignore the *warning signs* because we consider them as friends and associates and think we might never be affected by their behavior.

Be not deceived: evil communications corrupt good manners.[5]

Do not be deceived. You cannot have these types of friends and associates and think they will not affect you. Sooner or later, you will take their advice. Sooner or later, you will act as they do. Sooner or later, you too will mock others. It starts very small and grows as time goes on.

Though you might have invited these people into your life, they also invited you into theirs. And each time you overlook their questionable behavior, you increase the possibility you might take on their traits—slowly becoming ungodly, sinful, and scornful.

Deep down, you know you should have ended these friendships and associations a long time ago. These individuals are not trying to live godly or help you live godly. They want you to live as they do and might have encouraged you to do so. But for many reasons (e.g., fear of confrontation, loss of relationships, loneliness, etc.), you continued these relationships.

Along with friends and associates, consider media outlets, such as movies, television, and music. If you consider some of the most popular movies, television shows, and songs in society, they are filled with ungodly content, sinful actions, and scornful behavior. But much of this content is presented as *entertainment*, where we become desensitized to what we see or hear.

Many of us see so much murder on television and in movies that its effect on us is minimal when we read or hear about it in the news. Pre-marital sex and adultery are presented as beautiful encounters among two people rather than a great wickedness and

---

[5] 1 Corinthians 15:33.

sin against God.[6] Songs glorify all manner of sinful behavior, and yet, we allow its words to counsel our heart, soul, and mind. We hear comedians mock the poor, destitute, and those addicted to drugs and alcohol, and we laugh with them. We no longer consider that those individuals are hurting, want to be free, and are in need of help.[7]

These types of friends, associates, and media outlets cause us to lose sight of the people around us who are in need of a Savior. We become blind and numb to the things God hates.[8] We might forget, that as disciples of Jesus, we are to be a light, a voice of love and truth, and an example of holiness and righteousness unto God and others. We are His representatives in the world, laborers with Him to return His beautiful creation back to Him forever. This is the essence of the greatest commandments of loving God with all our heart, soul, and mind and loving our neighbor as ourselves.[9]

Being a disciple of Jesus is an all-or-nothing commitment.[10] But your friends, associates, and media outlets could be affecting your commitment to Him. You will need to decide who you will allow to be your teacher: Christ or the world...

---

[6] Genesis 39:9; 1 Corinthians 5:1–13, 6:12–20; Galatians 5:18–25; Ephesians 5:2–4.

[7] Matthew 9:35–38.

[8] Proverbs 3:31–32, 6:16–19, 15:26, 16:5, 20:23.

[9] Matthew 22:37–39.

[10] Luke 14:33; Revelation 3:14–22.

MEDITATE

But his delight is in the law of the Lord; and in his law doth he meditate day and night.[11]

To delight in God's word is to take pleasure in His word and consider it to be valuable, acceptable, and desirable. And when we have *this* delight, we would want to spend as much time with God's word as possible. Friends, associates, and media outlets that do not lead us along paths of godliness will not be a priority. We will remove ourselves from whatever keeps us from delighting ourselves in God's word so we can meditate on it day and night.

The bible translates *meditate* in Psalm 1:2 from the original Hebrew language as:

ponder—think about (something) carefully, especially before making a decision or reaching a conclusion

imagine—form a mental image or concept of

speak—say something in order to convey information, an opinion, or a feeling

---

[11] Psalm 1:2.

study—the devotion of time and attention to acquiring knowledge on an academic subject, especially by means of books; a detailed investigation and analysis of a subject or situation

talk—speak in order to give information or express ideas or feelings; converse or communicate by spoken words

Meditation is a daily experience of our thoughts, time, and communications. And as such, we should spend as many of the 1,440 minutes we receive each day pondering, imagining, speaking, studying, and talking about God's word.[12]

As God's word becomes your teacher, His message can shape your heart and life along paths of righteousness.[13] His word will guide you in the plan and purpose He has for your life. But you must also act on His word:

But be ye doers of the word, and not hearers only, deceiving your own selves. For if any be a hearer of the word, and not a doer, he is like unto a man beholding his natural face in a glass: For he beholdeth himself, and goeth his way, and straightway forgetteth what manner of man he was. But whoso looketh into the perfect law of liberty, and continueth therein, he being not a forgetful hearer, but a doer of the work, this man shall be blessed in his deed.[14]

When you continue looking into God's perfect law and carrying it out, you will be blessed in your work. This is the purpose of *Living for the Kingdom: Teaching What Jesus Taught*—to provide you with a guide to help you meditate on the commands of Jesus and teach you to obey them.

---

[12] Joshua 1:8; Psalm 119:9–11, 105.

[13] Psalm 23:3.

[14] James 1:22–25.

STUDY FORMATS

Before reading the first lesson, I want to share three formats you can use while studying *Living for the Kingdom: Teaching What Jesus Taught*.

Personal Study

Among the 115 lessons in this book, there are 79 separate topics. Each lesson is small enough to be studied daily, but please do not feel any pressure to move from one lesson to the next each day. Please take your time with each lesson and topic.

My recommendation is to spend one week on one topic. This allows you time to ponder, imagine, speak, study, and talk about the topic. With a one week, one topic approach, you will spend over eighteen months studying the commands of Jesus through this book.

Personal Study Format

There are many ways you can personally study *Living for the Kingdom: Teaching What Jesus Taught*. Following is one example you can consider within the weekly topic structure.

Preparation. As you begin your study, have your bible, study materials, and journal or application available (see Bible Study

Resources). The journal or application allows you to record your answers, thoughts, and convictions. Recording your answers, thoughts, and convictions provide a foundation for future individual and group study.

Prayer. Begin and end each study in prayer. Ask for God's help to prepare your heart and mind to hear from Him and be led into all truth.[15]

Heavenly Father, I thank You for this day You have given me. I thank You for the opportunity to study Your word and learn more about being a disciple of Jesus. I humbly ask for Your help to prepare my heart and mind to study this lesson today. Please allow my heart and mind to be at peace to hear from You. In the name of Jesus Christ I pray, Amen.

Read. Take the first moments of your study or the first day or two to read the scripture references within the topic lessons. You do not need to answer any lesson questions at this point. This is simply an opportunity for you to review the referenced scriptures. If you receive any thoughts or convictions about the scriptures, write them in your journal or application.

Meditate. Ponder, imagine, speak, study, and talk about the lessons within the topic throughout the week—*day and night.* Answer the questions within the topic, even if the topic covers multiple lessons. Take your time to review all applicable scripture references and include any answers, thoughts, or convictions in your journal or application.

---

[15] Matthew 7:7–11; John 16:13; 1 John 5:14–15.

Community Study

The second study format is the community study. *Living for the Kingdom: Teaching What Jesus Taught* is greatly beneficial in group settings. Community studies are founded on godly relationships. Godly relationships create the perfect environment for making disciples. Godly relationships are established in love[16] and built on honesty, openness, and trust,[17] encouragement,[18] selflessness,[19] graceful communications,[20] and wise counsel.[21] And through theses attributes, disciples can experience environments where God is glorified, God's Word is routinely discussed and used in practical application, godliness is encouraged and modeled, and an emphasis on making disciples is prominent.

Within the community study, each person can use the personal study format and come together on a specific day or throughout the week. The more a group can meet and talk together during the week, the greater the potential to strengthen their bonds of fellowship with one another and with Christ:

And they continued stedfastly in the apostles' doctrine and fellowship, and in breaking of bread, and in prayers. And fear came upon every soul: and many wonders and signs were done by the apostles. And all that believed were together, and had all things common; And sold their possessions and goods, and parted them to

---

[16] Proverbs 17:17; Matthew 22:36–40; Luke 6:31; John 13:34–35; 1 Corinthians 13:3–7; 1 John 3:18.

[17] Proverbs 16:28, 27:6; Romans 12:17; 2 Corinthians 4:1–7; Ephesians 4:25.

[18] Proverbs 27:17: Hebrews 3:12–13, 10:24–25.

[19] Romans 15:1; Philippians 2:4, 21.

[20] Ephesians 4:29, 5:4; Colossians 4:6.

[21] Proverbs 15:22, 27:9.

all men, as every man had need. And they, continuing daily with one accord in the temple, and breaking bread from house to house, did eat their meat with gladness and singleness of heart, Praising God, and having favour with all the people. And the Lord added to the church daily such as should be saved.[22]

The one recurring theme in Acts 2:42-47 is togetherness. The believers studied together, fellowshipped together, ate together, prayed together, went to church together (daily), remained together, and had all things in common. And as such, togetherness should be a foundational goal for your group study.

Whether you are eating together, bowling or playing cards, attending church services together, or sharing the highs and lows of life, you learn how to live as a disciple through word and deed, just as the twelve disciples had with Jesus.[23] Each group member is strengthened and encouraged to remain committed to God as you share your life and faith with one another.

Community Study Format

As your community of disciples meets together throughout the week, there are many ways you can establish meaningful conversations, exchanges, and experiences. You do not need a *formal* structure, but the following format is but one of many examples.

Meal. When meeting together, spend time in fellowship over a meal, beverage, or dessert. Create a relaxing atmosphere with open communication. There should be no specific boundaries on your discussions.

---

[22] Acts 2:42–47.

[23] John 13:1-17.

16

Prayer. As the meal concludes, begin your study in prayer. As you continue to meet, allow each person to have an opportunity to lead the group in prayer. Welcome Jesus into your study and open your hearts to the Holy Spirit.[24]

How is it then, brethren? when ye come together, every one of you hath a psalm, hath a doctrine, hath a tongue, hath a revelation, hath an interpretation. Let all things be done unto edifying.[25]

Open Mic. The Open Mic is a time for anyone in the group to share a psalm, scripture reading, song, or any other expression of the Gospel.

There might come a time when the Spirit leads your group to remain in the Open Mic period and not move into the study. Please do not become so intent on completing the lesson that you miss the Spirit's leading for edification, revelation, and grace to be shared.

Study. Like the personal study format, read the respective scripture references and work through the lesson questions. Before, during, and after completing the lesson questions, provide opportunities for each group member to share what they learned and experienced throughout the week. Before concluding, summarize your lesson comments and discussions and reinforce ways you can apply the lesson in your lives.

Prayer. Close your study in prayer. As you conclude, ask if anyone has any specific prayer requests. While praying, incorporate elements of the lesson topic and discussions.

---

[24] Matthew 18:20.

[25] 1 Corinthians 14:26.

Church Study

The church study encompasses elements of the personal and community studies. The church leader will use a lesson topic in the midweek bible study/service. For the weekend service, the church leader will share a corresponding message from the previous midweek bible study/service topic. Church members can study individually or in small groups to re-enforce the lesson material studied during the midweek bible study/service.

BIBLE STUDY RESOURCES

There are thousands of biblical resources to enhance your bible studies. This chapter will provide a sample of some of those resources.

Bible

The bible is the most important book ever written. It describes the beautiful creation of our world and everything contained therein. The pages of the bible reveal the beauty and depravity of humans and the gracious love and mercy of our Creator. And through God's love and mercy, we find salvation and eternal life through His son.

Because of the importance of the bible, you should look for a bible translation (or version) that helps you understand, apply, and communicate God's message. There are many different bible translations in today's marketplace.[26] Some translations are word-for-word or thought-for-thought translations, while others are paraphrases. Consider using a bible translation that is endorsed or used by your church, provides greater readability, or one God instructs you to use.

---

[26] The translations derive from the original languages of Hebrew and Aramaic (Old Testament) and Greek (New Testament).

Living for the Kingdom: Teaching What Jesus Taught uses the King James Bible as its source bible. Many of the lessons describe terms from the King James Bible that might be translated differently in another bible translation.

Bible Dictionary and Encyclopedia

Bible dictionaries and encyclopedias provide definitions and descriptions of biblical topics.

Easton's Bible Dictionary. Dr. Matthew George Easton (1823–1894) authored Easton's Bible Dictionary. It contains almost 4,000 entries relating to the bible.[27]

International Standard Bible Encyclopedia. James Orr (1844–1913) was the general editor of the International Standard Bible Encyclopedia. The encyclopedia contains articles from almost 200 scholars. The articles cover archaeological discoveries, the language and literature of bible lands, and the historical and religious environments of bible people.[28]

Bible Concordance

A bible concordance is an index of biblical words, often listed in alphabetical order.

Nave's Topical Bible. Orville James Nave (1841–1917), a chaplain in the United States Army, wrote Nave's Topical Bible. Nave's Topical Bible is a concordance with more than 20,000 biblical

[27] "Easton's Bible Dictionary," Wikipedia, Accessed June 22, 2014, http://en.m.wikipedia.org/wiki/Easton's_Bible_Dictionary.

[28] "International Standard Bible Encyclopedia," Wikipedia, Accessed June 22, 2014, http://en.m.wikipedia.org/wiki/ International_Standard_Bible_Encyclopedia.

topics. It also includes more than 10,000 scripture quotations indexed according to topic.[29]

Strong's Concordance. Dr. James Strong (1822–1894) published Strong's Concordance in 1890. Strong's Concordance defines every Hebrew and Greek word in the King James Bible.[30] Strong's Concordance provides an independent cross-check when using or comparing bible translations. It offers the opportunity for an accurate understanding of the biblical text.[31]

Treasury of Scripture Knowledge. The Treasury of Scripture Knowledge provides more than 500,000 biblical cross-references.[32] The cross-references are an index of thoughts and ideas, not exact matches.[33] It also includes book summaries, chapter outlines, and alternative readings.[34]

Young's Analytical Concordance to the Bible. Robert Young (1822–1888) published Young's Analytical Concordance to the Bible in 1879. This concordance is suited for word studies. It

---

[29] "Nave's Topical Bible," Wikipedia, Accessed June 22, 2014, http://en.m.wikipedia.org/wiki/Nave%E2%80%99s_Topical_Bible.

[30] Dr. Strong treated Hebrew and Aramaic as one language.

[31] "Strong's Concordance," Wikipedia, Accessed June 22, 2014, https://en.wikipedia.org/wiki/Strong%27s_Concordance.

[32] "Treasury of Scripture Knowledge," Bible Study Tools, Accessed December 1, 2016, http://www.biblestudytools.com/concordances/treasury-of-scripture-knowledge/.

[33] "TSK Help Tutorial," Blue Letter Bible, Accessed December 1, 2016, https://www.blueletterbible.org/help/tsk.cfm.

[34] "The Treasury of Scripture Knowledge: Expanded with 800,000 Cross-References," SwordSearcher, Accessed December 1, 2016, http://www.swordsearcher.com/bible-study-library/treasury-of-scripture-knowledge.html.

analyzes English words and lists scriptures containing each corresponding Hebrew or Greek word.[35]

Bible Commentary

Bible commentaries are a form of biblical exegesis (or explanation). They provide explanations of biblical passages and books of the bible.

Matthew Henry's Complete Bible Commentary. This concordance provides an exhaustive verse-by-verse study of the bible.[36]

Bible Software and Websites

Bible software and websites provide libraries of biblical resources. They offer several ways to understand, apply, and communicate God's word.

YouVersion. YouVersion is the ministry of Life.Church. YouVersion's purpose is to provide a free bible for every phone, tablet, and computer in the world.[37] Through its website, Bible.com, and application, YouVersion provides over 1,400 bible translations supporting 1,071 languages.[38]

---

[35] "Young's Analytical Concordance to the Bible," Wikipedia, Accessed December 8, 2016, https://en.wikipedia.org/wiki/Young's_Analytical_Concordance_to_the_Bible.

[36] "Matthew Henry," Wikipedia, Accessed June 22, 2014, http://en.wikipedia.org/wiki/Matthew_Henry.

[37] "Resources & Applications for Churches | Life.Church," Life.Church, Accessed January 25, 2017, http:// www.life.church/churches/?utm_ source=life.church.

[38] "YouVersion" YouVersion, Accessed January 25, 2017, https://www.youversion.com.

e-Sword. e-Sword is a bible study application and computer program created by Rick Meyers in 2000. e-Sword provides bible translations, a reference library, audio sermons, and much more.[39]

Bible Gateway. Nick Hengeveld created Bible Gateway in 1993. Bible Gateway provides a website and application with over 50 bible translations, advanced search tools, and other biblical resources.[40]

Bible Hub. Bible Hub began as an online platform in 2004 through the Online Parallel Bible Project. Bible Hub has a three-purpose mission:

1. increase the visibility and accessibility of the scriptures online,

2. provide free access to bible study tools in many languages,

3. promote the Gospel through the learning, study, and application of God's word.[41]

Blue Letter Bible. The Blue Letter Bible Project is an initiative of Sowing Circle Ministries. Blue Letter Bible provides three ongoing initiatives:

1. CDs for missionaries, pastors, and students,

2. a website for online bible studies,

---

[39] "Features," e-Sword, Accessed November 29, 2016, http://www.e-sword.net/index.html#features.

[40] "BibleGateway.com," Wikipedia, Accessed November 29, 2016, https://en.wikipedia.org/wiki/BibleGateway.com.

[41] "About Us," Bible Hub, Accessed November 29, 2016, http://biblehub.com/about.htm.

3. an institute for structured biblical studies.[42]

OpenBible.info. OpenBible.info provides several biblical resources, such as a topical bible, bible maps, and cross-references of the bible. OpenBible.info also provides a *lab* with small experiments using biblical data.

---

[42] "Blue Letter Bible," Wikipedia, Accessed November 29, 2016, https://en.wikipedia.org/wiki/Blue_Letter_Bible.

LESSON OUTLINE

1

Cost of Discipleship

Luke 14:25–33

When someone comes to Jesus, who must he or she hate in order to be His disciple (Luke 14:26)?

What does it mean to take up your cross (Romans 6:1–7:19; Galatians 2:19–20, Galatians 5:22–24; Ephesians 4:22–25; Philippians 2:1–11; Colossians 3:1–25; Titus 2:11–14)?

Describe the scenarios of the builder and king in Luke 14:28–32. What did they need to consider before proceeding?

What do you need to consider in order to be a disciple of Jesus (Luke 14:33)?

2

Cost of Discipleship

Matthew 8:1–22

Look up *scribe* in a bible dictionary or encyclopedia.

Reading Matthew 8:18–20, how did Jesus' statement to the scribe challenge his current lifestyle?

A disciple told Jesus he wanted to first bury his father before following Him. Jesus responded by saying '*let the dead bury their own dead*.' Why would Jesus refer to the living as dead (Romans 8:6–9; Colossians 2:13; Ephesians 2:1–5)?

What does Matthew 8:18–22 say about the *cost* of following Jesus?

3

Cost of Discipleship

Matthew 10:1–39

Do you believe Jesus came to earth to send peace? How could Jesus' statement in Matthew 10:34 challenge a person's thinking (2 Peter 3:6–10; Revelation 19:1–21:1)?

Why would there be divisions within a family (Matthew 10:16–22, 35–36)?

How can someone be worthy of Jesus?

In what two ways can a person *lose* his or her life (Luke 12:14–31; Galatians 5:19–21; James 4:4; 1 John 2:15–17)? What will he or she find?

4

Cost of Discipleship

Mark 8:34–38 and Luke 9:23–27

Discuss the profit and loss in Mark 8:35–38 and Luke 9:24–25.

What does it mean to be ashamed of Jesus and His words (Matthew 10:32–33; Luke 9:26)?

Look up *ashamed* in a bible dictionary or Strong's Concordance (#G1870).

What will happen to those who are ashamed of Jesus and His words?

How can you not be ashamed of Jesus and His words (Romans 1:16; 2 Timothy 1:8–14; 1 John 2:28)?

5

Beatitudes

Matthew 5:3 and Luke 6:20
(review Matthew 5:1–12 and Luke 6:17–26)

The nine beatitudes represent the character traits or behaviors a person attains on earth in order to enter eternal life (the kingdom of heaven).

Being poor in spirit is being poor in stature (humility).

Look up *humility* in a bible dictionary.

Read Luke 18:9–14 to find an example of being poor in spirit (stature, humility).

What will the poor in spirit receive?

In Luke 6:20, who did Jesus say was blessed?

Review the contrast between Luke 6:20 and Luke 6:24.

Read Mark 10:17-25 and James 2:5-7 to read examples of the rich.

Can a person serve God and wealth (Matthew 6:24)?

6

Beatitudes

Matthew 5:4–5 and Luke 6:25
(review Matthew 5:1–12 and Luke 6:17–26)

Look up *mourn* in Strong's Concordance (#G3996).

Summarize Ecclesiastes 7:2–4 and Revelation 21:2–4.

Look up *meek* in Strong's Concordance (#G4239).

What is the opposite of *meek*? Also, review the following scriptures: Proverbs 25:6–8, Proverbs 27:1–2; Luke 14:8–11.

Read Psalm 22:26, Psalm 25:8–10, Psalm 37:7–11, Psalm 147:6, Psalm 149:4; 2 Timothy 2:24–26.

7

Beatitudes

Matthew 5:6–7 and Luke 6:21a
(review Matthew 5:1–12 and Luke 6:17–26)

Define *hunger* and *thirst* in a dictionary.

Look up *righteousness* in Strong's Concordance (#G1343).

Putting these together, what does it mean to hunger and thirst for righteousness?

In what ways will the righteous be filled (Matthew 25:31–46; Hebrews 11 (specifically verses 13–16); Revelation 21:1–8)?

Look up *mercy* or *merciful* in a bible dictionary.

Based on Matthew 18:21–35 and Matthew 25:31–46, in what ways can you receive mercy? What will occur if you do not show mercy to others?

8

Beatitudes

Matthew 5:8–12
(review Matthew 5:1–12 and Luke 6:17–26)

Look up *pure* (#G2513) and *heart* (#G2588) in Strong's Concordance.

How can your heart be defiled (Matthew 15:1–20; Mark 7:1–23)?

How can your heart be cleansed (Psalm 51:1–17, Psalm 119:1–17; James 4:7–10)?

Look up *peacemaker* in Strong's Concordance (#G1518). What does it mean to be a peacemaker?

Name a few ways you can be a peacemaker in your home, church, and workplace (Matthew 5:43–48; Luke 6:27–35; Romans 8:13–17).

Reading Matthew 5:10–12 and Luke 6:22–23, who are those that are blessed?

9

Salt

Matthew 5:13, Mark 9:42–50,
and Luke 14:34–35

Look up *salt* in a bible dictionary.

What are disciples to have in themselves and with one another (Mark 9:50)?

In what ways can you be the salt of the earth (Matthew 7:24–27; Romans 12:1–2; Ephesians 4:17–32)?

What is salt good for if it loses its savor (Matthew 5:13; Luke 14:34–35)?

10

Light

Matthew 5:14–16

Look up *light* in Strong's Concordance (#G5457).

Explain the examples Jesus illustrates in Matthew 5:14–16.

Why should you shine your light before men (1 Corinthians 10:31; Philippians 2:14–16; 1 Peter 4:10–11)?

11

Light

Mark 4:21–23 and Luke 8:16–18

What will happen with secrets and hidden things?

How will your works and deeds be exposed (Matthew 25:31–46; 1 Corinthians 3:10–15, 1 Corinthians 4:1–5)?

Read John 1:6–14 and John 3:19–21. Who hates the light? Who comes to the light? Why do people come to the light? What will coming to the light show?

How should you live as a disciple (1 Peter 1:13–25)?

12

Light

Matthew 6:22–23 and Luke 11:33–36

What is the light of the body?

Look up *single* in Strong's Concordance (#G573).

How do you become full of light or darkness?

What warning did Jesus give about darkness?

Can you have some darkness and be full of light?

13

Law and Commandments

Matthew 5:17–20 and Luke 16:16–17

What does Jesus say about His coming (Matthew 5:17)?

What does Jesus say about the law and the prophets?

Look up *Law of Moses* in a bible dictionary and read a bible commentary on Matthew 5:17.

It is easier for heaven and earth to pass away than for what to occur?

Look up *tittle* in Strong's Concordance (#G2762).

Who is considered least and great in the kingdom of heaven?

14

Law and Commandments

Matthew 5:17–20 and Luke 16:16–17

Look up *Pharisee* in a bible dictionary.

How can you enter the kingdom of heaven?

Read Matthew 15:1–20 and Matthew 23:1–36 for two examples of the righteousness of scribes and Pharisees.

How can your righteousness exceed the scribes and Pharisees (Matthew 7:24–25; John 5:24, John 8:51; James 1:21–27; 1 John 2:17)?

15

Anger and Conflict

Matthew 5:21–26

When Jesus told the disciples, '*ye have heard that it was said of them of old time...*,' what was He referring to (Exodus 20:13 and Deuteronomy 5:17)?

Look up *judgment* in Strong's Concordance (#G2920).

How can you be in danger of judgment, the Council, or hell fire (Matthew 5:21–22)?

Look up *raca* in Strong's Concordance (#G4469).

What should happen if you bring a gift to the altar and remember that someone has something against you?

16

Anger and Conflict

Matthew 5:21–26

Look up *adversary* in Strong's Concordance (#G476).

Why should you agree with your adversary quickly?

Look up *farthing* in Strong's Concordance (#G2835).

Read a bible commentary on Matthew 5:21–26.

17

Adultery
and Lust

Matthew 5:27–32 and Luke 16:18

When Jesus told the disciples, '*ye have heard that it was said by them of old time...*,' what was He referring to (Exodus 20:14; Deuteronomy 5:18)?

Look up *adultery* and *lust* in a bible dictionary.

In what ways can you commit adultery?

Where is the offense of adultery committed? Read Mark 7:14–23 as well.

Look up *offend* in Strong's Concordance (#G4624).

What should you do with your right eye or hand if it offends you? Why?

18

Marriage
and Divorce

*Matthew 5:31–32, Matthew 19:1–12,
Mark 10:1–12, and Luke 16:18*

What does Jesus say about marriage in Matthew 19:4–6 and Mark 10:6–9?

When two people are married, what do they become (Genesis 2:18–25)?

What does Jesus say about those God joins together in marriage?

Read Proverbs 5, Proverbs 18:22; Ephesians 5:22–33; Colossians 3:18–19; 1 Thessalonians 5:18; Titus 2; 1 Peter 3:1–12.

19

Marriage and Divorce

Matthew 5:31–32, Matthew 19:1–12,
Mark 10:1–12, and Luke 16:18

When Jesus told the disciples, '*it hath been said...*' in Matthew 5:31, what was He referring to (Deuteronomy 24:1–4)?

Why did Moses permit divorce?

Why did Jesus say a man could divorce his wife? What happens if the divorce is for any other reason? What will happen to the person who marries a divorcee under those circumstances?

What is the consequence for those who commit adultery (Leviticus 20:10; Mark 7:20–23; Galatians 5:19–21)?

20

Oaths
and Vows

Matthew 5:33–37

Look up *oath* and *vow* in a bible dictionary.

What did Jesus say about those of old time (Leviticus 19:12)?

What are you not to swear by? Why?

If you cannot swear, what should you do (James 5:12)?

What happens if you go beyond what Jesus said?

21

Give and Take

Matthew 5:38–42 and Luke 6:27–36

When Jesus told the disciples, '*ye have heard that it was said…,*' what was He referring to (Exodus 21:22–24; Leviticus 24:17–22; Deuteronomy 19:15–21)?

How should you deal with evil people or someone wanting to sue you or compel you to go one mile?

How should you respond to someone who begs of you or wants to borrow something? Should you expect what was borrowed to be returned?

How should you respond to someone who takes from you?

Read Leviticus 19:18; Proverbs 20:22, Proverbs 24:17–18, Proverbs 24:29, Proverbs 25:21–22; Romans 12:14, Romans 12:17–21.

22

Love and Mercy

Matthew 5:43–48 and Luke 6:27–36

Should you only love the people who love you? Please explain.

How can you be children of your Father in heaven (children of the Highest)? Describe each example Jesus illustrates. What will you receive?

How does God treat the unthankful, evil, just, and unjust?

What does Jesus say about mercy?

Review your responses from Lesson 7 on mercy.

23

Giving

Matthew 6:1–4 and Luke 6:38

What are alms? Look up *alms* in Strong's Concordance (#G1654).

Why would someone give his or her alms in front of people?

How were the hypocrites giving their alms?

What reward did the hypocrites receive?

How did Jesus say you should give alms? Who will reward you? Where (and how) will your reward be given?

24

Prayer

Matthew 6:5–13, Luke 11:1–4,
and Luke 18:1–8

How do hypocrites pray? Why?

What reward will hypocrites receive?

How should you pray to your Father? What reward will you receive?

How do heathens pray? Why?

Why should you not pray like the heathen?

25

Prayer

Matthew 6:5–13, Luke 11:1–4,
and Luke 18:1–8

Please read the following commentary and scripture references:

Our Father which art in heaven, Hallowed be thy name.[43]

As we enter into prayer, we acknowledge our Father who is in heaven. Hallowed (holy, set apart) is His Name. Our Father is to be honored, worshipped, and revered within our minds, hearts, and lips.

Thy kingdom come, Thy will be done in earth, as it is in heaven.[44]

We pray for the kingdom of God to come and God's will to be done. As we pray for God's kingdom to come, we are asking for His kingdom to be advanced around the world by His Spirit. With the kingdom of God within us (in our hearts), we live in conformity to God's standard and not our nature in the flesh.[45]

---

[43] Matthew 6:9.

[44] Matthew 6:10.

[45] Luke 17:20–21.

Give us this day our daily bread.[46]

We ask God for our daily substance—what is needed for today, and not the next day, month, or year. We do not ask for too much where we forget God or too little where we steal.[47] We trust God to provide what we need.[48]

And forgive us our debts, as we forgive our debtors.[49]

We ask God to forgive us for our sins as we forgive those who sin against us! Holding unto unforgiveness places our eternal lives with God at risk:

For if ye forgive men their trespasses, your heavenly Father will also forgive you: But if ye forgive not men their trespasses, neither will your Father forgive your trespasses.[50]

Lead us not into temptation, but deliver us from evil: For thine is the kingdom, and the power, and the glory, for ever.[51]

As Jesus acknowledges that the Spirit is willing, and the flesh is weak,[52] we must trust God to show us a way of escape from temptation...*and take it!*[53]

---

[46] Matthew 6:11.

[47] Proverbs 30:7–9; Matthew 6:25–34.

[48] Matthew 6:8.

[49] Matthew 6:12.

[50] Matthew 6:14–15.

[51] Matthew 6:13.

[52] Matthew 26:36–46.

[53] John 17:15; 1 Corinthians 10:13; 2 Thessalonians 3:1–3; 2 Timothy 4:18.

In concluding our prayer, we acknowledge that the kingdom (rule), power (ability), and glory (honor, exaltation, and preeminence) are God's forever. We are reminded of His place within our lives, this earth, and the one to come.[54]

---

[54] Revelation 21:1–8.

26

Prayer

*Matthew 6:5–13, Luke 11:1–4,
and Luke 18:1–8*

Why did Jesus share the parable in Luke 18:1–8?

How was the judge described?

What did the widow ask the judge? For how long?

What was his initial response?

Why did the judge grant the widow's request?

27

Prayer

Matthew 6:5–13, Luke 11:1–4,
and Luke 18:1–8

What does the elect do before God (Luke 18:7)? What will the Lord do for His elect?

What does it mean to '*bear long with them*' (Luke 18:7)?

Look up *bear* in Strong's Concordance (#G3114).

Jesus makes a statement about the Son of man's coming. Who is the Son of man? Look up *Son of man* in a bible dictionary.

When will the Son of man come (Matthew 24; Luke 17:22–37)?

28

Forgiveness

Matthew 6:14–15, Matthew 18:21–35,
Mark 11:25–26, Luke 7:36–50,
and Luke 17:3–10

What will happen if you forgive someone for the sins he or she commits against you (Matthew 6:14–15)?

What will happen if you do not forgive him or her?

Are there any people in your life (past or present) who have wronged you and you have not forgiven?

Please consider your life circumstances in view of Jesus' words in Matthew 6:14–15. If unforgiveness exists in your life, pray about your thoughts, fears, and concerns so you may begin a process of healing and forgiveness.

29

Forgiveness

Matthew 6:14–15, Matthew 18:21–35,
Mark 11:25–26, Luke 7:36–50,
and Luke 17:3–10

When Peter asked how many times he should forgive his brother who sins against him, what was Jesus' response (Matthew 18:21)? Compare with Luke 17:3–4 as well.

Jesus shares a parable in Matthew 18:23–35. What is He describing (Matthew 18:23)?

Summarize Matthew 18:23–35.

30

Forgiveness

Matthew 6:14–15, Matthew 18:21–35,
Mark 11:25–26, Luke 7:36–50,
and Luke 17:3–10

How much is ten thousand talents worth? Look up *talent* and *weight* or *weights and measurements* in a bible dictionary.

How much is one hundred pence? Look up #G1220 in Strong's Concordance.

Compare what each servant owed.

Why was the servant considered wicked (Matthew 18:32–33)?

What is the *moral* of the parable (Matthew 18:22, Matthew 18:33, Matthew 18:35)?

How are you to forgive others (Matthew 18:35)?

31

Fasting

*Matthew 6:16–18, Matthew 9:14–17,
Matthew 17:14–21, Mark 2:18–22,
Mark 9:17–29, and Luke 5:33–39*

How do hypocrites fast?

Who do hypocrites fast to? What reward do hypocrites receive?

How should you fast?

Who do you fast for (review Luke 2:36–37; Acts 13:1–3 as well)?
What reward will you receive?

32

Fasting

Matthew 6:16–18, Matthew 9:14–17,
Matthew 17:14–21, Mark 2:18–22,
Mark 9:17–29, and Luke 5:33–39

Who came to Jesus to ask why His disciples do not fast (Matthew 9:14–17; Mark 2:18–22; Luke 5:33–39)? Who were they comparing Jesus' disciples to?

Who are the children of the bridechamber? Look up *children of the bridechamber*, *bridegroom*, and *marriage* in a bible encyclopedia.

Who is the bridegroom (John 3:29)?

What emotion is associated with fasting (Matthew 9:15)? Look up this emotion in Strong's Concordance (#G3996).

When will Jesus' disciples fast?

33

Fasting

Matthew 6:16–18, Matthew 9:14–17,
Matthew 17:14–21, Mark 2:18–22,
Mark 9:17–29, and Luke 5:33–39

What two different types of materials are listed in Matthew 9:16–17? Look up *wine-skins* or *wineskin* in a bible dictionary. Why can there not be a mix of the two? How are they preserved?

When the bridegroom is taken from the disciples, what are some of the things to occur (John 14:1–6; Acts 2; Romans 6:1–4; 2 Corinthians 5:17; Revelation 21:1–8)?

Read a bible commentary on Matthew 9:14–17.

34

Fasting

Matthew 6:16–18, Matthew 9:14–17,
Matthew 17:14–21, Mark 2:18–22,
Mark 9:17–29, and Luke 5:33–39

Who came to Jesus in Matthew 17:14–21 and Mark 9:17–29?

What were they asking Him to do? Why?

How was unbelief and faithlessness a factor?

How did Jesus *answer* their requests?

What did Jesus' disciples ask Him (Matthew 17:19)?

Certain spirits can only come out in what two ways (Matthew 17:20–21; Mark 9:29)?

35

Treasures in
Heaven and Earth

*Matthew 6:19–21, Luke 12:13–21,
and Luke 12:31–34*

Summarize Luke 12:13–21.

Where can treasures be placed? How is each location described?

Why is the location of your treasure important (Matthew 6:21;
Luke 12:34)?

How can you lay up treasures in heaven (Matthew 25:31–46; Luke
12:33)?

36

Worry

Matthew 6:25–34 and Luke 12:22–34

What five things does Jesus say you are not to take any thought for?

What is more important than *meat* and *raiment*?

Look up *raiment* in a bible dictionary.

What does Jesus say about the fowls of the air (Matthew 6:26)? How are they fed? How are you compared to them?

Can worrying about the five things above add to your stature (Matthew 6:27)?

Look up *stature* in Strong's Concordance (#G2244).

37

Worry

Matthew 6:25–34 and Luke 12:22–34

What does Jesus say about taking *thought for raiment* (Matthew 6:28–29)?

Describe Solomon's glory (1 Kings 10). What was greater than Solomon's glory on earth?

If God clothed the grass of the field, what will He do for you?

If you should not worry about these things, what two things should you do (Matthew 6:33)? What will you receive?

Why should not you take any thought for what might occur tomorrow (Matthew 6:34)?

38

Judging Others

Matthew 7:1–5

What does it mean to judge someone? Look up *judge* in Strong's Concordance (#G2919).

What would happen if you judge someone (Matthew 7:2)?

Look up *mote* and *beam* in a bible dictionary.

In order to help someone remove the *mote* from his or her eye, what must you do first?

Based on Jesus' examples in Matthew 7:1–5, is it okay to help others *see* the issues in their lives? Would that be the same as judging them?

39

Pearls
Among Swine
Matthew 7:6

Look up the Hebrew and Greek words for *dogs* (#H3611, G2965) and *swine* (#H2386, G5519) in Strong's Concordance.

What are you not to give to dogs or cast unto swine? Why?

What does it mean to rend something? Look up *rend* in Strong's Concordance (#G4486).

Read a bible commentary on Matthew 7:6.

40

Ask, Seek, Knock

Matthew 7:7–12 and Luke 11:5–13

In what three ways can you receive answers from your Father in heaven?

How does Jesus compare an earthly father to your Father in heaven?

How should you treat others (Matthew 7:12; Matthew 22:36–40; Galatians 5:14)?

Read a bible commentary on Matthew 7:7–12.

41

Ask, Seek, Knock

Matthew 7:7–12 and Luke 11:5–13

Summarize Luke 11:5–8.

Look up *importunity* in Strong's Concordance (#G335) and a bible dictionary.

What will your heavenly Father give to those who ask?

42

Wide and
Strait Gates

Matthew 7:13–14 and Luke 13:22–30

Describe the two gates. Where does each gate lead?

Who enters through the wide and strait gates (Luke 13:24, 27)?

What does it mean to strive to enter the strait gate? Look up *strive* in Strong's Concordance (#G75).

Read a bible commentary on Luke 13:22–30.

43

Good and
Bad Fruit

*Matthew 7:15–20, Matthew 12:33–37,
and Luke 6:43–45*

Who should you beware of? How do they come to you? What is their true nature?

How will you recognize them?

Describe the two types of fruits and trees. What type of comparison/contrast is being made?

What happens to trees that do not produce good fruit?

Describe the difference between good and evil men. What determines the content of their speech?

Why should you be cautious of the words you use?

Read Matthew 16:24–28; Acts 17:16–31; 2 Corinthians 5:10; Revelation 20:11–15.

44

Doing God's Will

Matthew 7:21–27 and Luke 6:46–49

Will everyone enter the kingdom of heaven (Matthew 7:21)? Who will enter?

Many will not enter the kingdom of heaven. What will they say to the Lord? What did they do in His name (Matthew 7:22)?

What will Jesus say in response (Matthew 7:23)? Why?

Look up *iniquity* in Strong's Concordance (#G458) or a bible dictionary.

Who can enter the kingdom of heaven?

45

House Foundations

Matthew 7:24–27 and Luke 6:46–49

Where did the foolish and wise men build their houses?

What made them foolish or wise?

How was each house *tested*?

What was the final outcome of their houses?

46

Harvest Workers

Matthew 9:35–38 and Luke 10:1–2
(read verses 1–20 for context)

What was Jesus doing in the cities and villages?

Look up *gospel* in Strong's Concordance (#G2098).

What happened when Jesus saw the multitudes?

Look up *sheep*, *shepherd*, and *harvest* in a bible encyclopedia.

What did Jesus tell the disciples to do?

Who is the Lord of the harvest (Matthew 9:37–38, Matthew 13:24–30, Matthew 13:36–43; Luke 10:1–20)?

What is the harvest comprised of?

In what two ways do laborers work in the Lord's harvest?

47

Preparing Disciples

Matthew 10, Mark 6:7–13,
Luke 9:1–6, and John 15:18–21

Who were the twelve disciples Jesus called to Himself?

Look up *apostle* in a bible dictionary.

What type of power did Jesus give the twelve disciples?

Look up the names of each disciple in a bible dictionary or encyclopedia.

48

Preparing Disciples

Matthew 10, Mark 6:7–13,
Luke 9:1–6, and John 15:18–21

When Jesus sent out the twelve disciples, where did He tell them to go (and not go)?

What message did Jesus give the disciples to speak?

What additional instructions did Jesus give the disciples (Matthew 10:8–14; Mark 6:7–13; Luke 9:1–6)?

What did Jesus send the disciples out as (Matthew 10:16)? Consider the contrasts Jesus gives while reviewing the following scriptures: Genesis 3:1; Romans 16:16–19; Philippians 2:14–15.

49

Preparing Disciples

Matthew 10, Mark 6:7–13,
Luke 9:1–6, and John 15:18–21

What did Jesus tell the disciples to beware of (Matthew 10:17)? Why?

Look up *council, scourge,* and *synagogue* in a bible dictionary.

Name the two reasons disciples will be brought before governors and kings.

What comfort did Jesus promise the disciples when they would be brought before governors and kings (Matthew 10:19–20)?

50

Preparing Disciples

Matthew 10, Mark 6:7–13,
Luke 9:1–6, and John 15:18–21

How can a disciple be persecuted by his or her family and community (Matthew 10:21–23)?

Look up *persecution* in a bible dictionary or encyclopedia.

In the face of persecution, what must disciples do to the end in order to be saved?

In Matthew 10:24–25, Jesus speaks on the relationship between the disciple and servant and his master and lord. Describe the relationships. Who is the disciples' master and lord?

Read Matthew 5:10–12; Luke 6:39–41; John 13:1–17, John 15:19–27; Romans 8:12–29; 2 Timothy 2:3–5, 2 Timothy 3:10–17; 1 Peter 5:6–11.

Look up *Beelzebub* in a bible dictionary.

51

Preparing Disciples

Matthew 10, Mark 6:7–13,
Luke 9:1–6, and John 15:18–21

What are the three *fear not* statements Jesus provides (Matthew 10:26–31)?

What will happen to things that are covered and hid? Read Matthew 12:35–36; 1 Corinthians 3:1–15, 1 Corinthians 4:1–5.

Describe Jesus' comparison between the sparrows and His disciples.

How much is a sparrow sold for? Look up *farthing* in a bible dictionary.

Does your Father know everything that happens in the world and to you? Read Psalm 139; Proverbs 15:3; Matthew 10:29–30.

52

Preparing Disciples

Matthew 10, Mark 6:7–13,
Luke 9:1–6, and John 15:18–21

What promise exists for those who confess and deny Jesus before men (Matthew 10:32–33)?

What did the disciples accomplish when they were sent out (Mark 6:7–13; Luke 9:1–6)?

What did the disciples say to Jesus when they returned? What did Jesus do next (Mark 6:30–32; Luke 9:10)?

53

The Sabbath

Matthew 12:1–14, Mark 2:23–28,
Luke 6:1–11, Luke 13:10–17,
John 5:1–16, and John 9

According to the Pharisees, scribes, ruler of the synagogue, and Jews, what *unlawful* acts was Jesus (or others) committing on the Sabbath? List their accusations.

Look up *Sabbath* in a bible dictionary.

What does the Law of Moses say about the Sabbath and work (Exodus 16, Exodus 31:15; Numbers 15:32–36)?

Who is Lord of the Sabbath (Mark 2:28; Luke 6:5)?

54

The Sabbath

Matthew 12:1–14, Mark 2:23–28,
Luke 6:1–11, Luke 13:10–17,
John 5:1–16, and John 9

In response to the Pharisees in Matthew 12:3–5, what two examples did Jesus provide?

In the examples Jesus provided, why was David and the Pharisees not in violation of breaking God's commands (Matthew 9:9–13, Matthew 12:7)?

What is lawful to do on the Sabbath (Matthew 12:12; Luke 6:9–10, Luke 13:10–17)?

Who was the Sabbath made for (Mark 2:27)?

Read a bible commentary on Matthew 12:1–14.

55

Blasphemy of the Holy Spirit

*Matthew 12:22–37, Mark 3:22–30,
Luke 11:14–28, and Luke 12:10*

What type of devil did Jesus heal the man from in Matthew 12:22 and Luke 11:14?

What were some of the responses from the people (including Pharisees)?

By what spirit (power, authority) did the people (and Pharisees) say Jesus was using to cast out devils?

What three things did Jesus say could not be divided against itself? Why?

How can a strong man's house be spoiled? Look up *spoiled* in Strong's Concordance (#G1283).

56

Blasphemy of the Holy Spirit

Matthew 12:22–37, Mark 3:22–30,
Luke 11:14–28, and Luke 12:1

What happens to those who are not with Jesus or gathers with Him (Matthew 12:30)?

Read Matthew 4:19, Matthew 28:18–20; John 8:31–32, John 13:35; Acts 11:25–26; 1 Corinthians 3:5–9.

Can men be forgiven from every type of sin (Matthew 12:31–32; Mark 3:28–30)? Please explain.

Look up *blasphemy* in Strong's Concordance (#G988).

57

Blasphemy of the Holy Spirit

Matthew 12:22–37, Mark 3:22–30,
Luke 11:14–28, and Luke 12:1

Where does an unclean spirit go when it is gone out of a man (Luke 11:24–28)?

If the unclean spirit does not find another place to go, what does it decide to do?

What is the state of the man if the spirits enter into him?

After Jesus finished speaking, what did a woman in the group say to Him? What did Jesus say in response?

Review one of the scripture references in a bible commentary.

58

Showing Signs

Matthew 12:38–42, Matthew 16:1–4,
and Mark 8:11–12

What did the Pharisees ask Jesus?

What is a *sign*? Look up *sign* in a bible encyclopedia.

Why did some people seek signs from Jesus (Matthew 16:1–4; John 4:46–54; 1 Corinthians 1:18–25)?

What sign did Jesus say would be given?

For the sign concerning Jonah, where would Jesus be? Read the book of Jonah for context, then read Matthew 17:22–23 and Mark 8:31.

Review your comments from 1 Kings 10 in Lesson 37 (Worry).

59

Parable of the Sower

*Matthew 13:1–23, Mark 4:1–20,
and Luke 8:4–15*

What does the seed in this parable represent (Mark 4:14; Luke 8:11)?

Create a chart with three columns: Location, Result, and Meaning.

Where did the seeds land? Place responses under Location.

What was the result of each seed? Place responses under Result.

What meaning did Jesus assign to each of the seeds? Place responses under Meaning.

How can seeds be planted in good soil (Matthew 13:23; Mark 4:20; Luke 8:15)?

60

Parable of the Tares of the Field

Matthew 13:24–30 and Matthew 13:36–43

What was Jesus describing in this parable (Matthew 13:24)?

What did the man plant in his field? What did the enemy do in the man's field? What was the result?

What did the servants of the householder discover? What did the servants of the householder want to do?

What did the householder say about gathering the tares?

What would happen to the wheat if it was gathered before the harvest (Matthew 13:29)?

When will the wheat and tares be gathered?

What will happen to the wheat and tares at the harvest?

61

Parable of the Tares of the Field

Matthew 13:24–30 and Matthew 13:36–43

Who sows the good seed?

Who represents the good seed?

Who represents the tares?

What is the field?

Explain what will occur at the harvest.

What will happen to those who offend and do iniquity?

What will be the end state of the righteous?

62

Parable of the Mustard Seed

Matthew 13:31–32, Mark 4:30–32,
and Luke 13:18–19

What did Jesus compare the kingdom of heaven to?

Look up *mustard seed* in a bible encyclopedia.

Describe Jesus' depiction of the beginning state of a mustard seed.
What happens to the mustard seed when it grows?

What will the mustard seed provide once it grows?

Read Luke 17:20–21. What will happen when the kingdom of God
grows within you (Matthew 22:36–40, Matthew 25:31–40; John
13:35, John 14:15–17; Acts 1:1–8)?

What else will the kingdom of heaven provide (John 14:23; Romans
14:17; Revelation 21)?

63

Parable of the Leaven

Matthew 13:33 and Luke 13:20–21

What did Jesus compare the kingdom of heaven to?

Look up *leaven* in a bible encyclopedia.

After reviewing Lesson 62, how can *leaven* (the kingdom of heaven) have an impact on people and the world?

Read Matthew 16:5–11 and 1 Corinthians 5:7–8.

64

Parable of the Hidden Treasure and Merchant

Matthew 13:44–46

When the man found the treasure, how did he react?

How valuable was the treasure compared to his other possessions?

When the merchantman found the pearl of great price, what did he do?

Did the price of the pearl deter the merchantman from wanting to purchase it?

In comparison, how valuable is the kingdom of heaven?

65

Parable of the Fishing Net

Matthew 13:47–52

What did Jesus compare the kingdom of heaven to?

What will happen to the good and bad?

After speaking to His disciples, what did Jesus ask if they understood (Matthew 13:36–50)?

Read a bible commentary on Matthew 13:47–52.

66

Greatest in the Kingdom

Matthew 18:1–6, Matthew 19:13–14,
Mark 9:33–37, Mark 10:13–16,
Luke 9:46–48, and Luke 18:15–17

What question did Jesus answer in Matthew 18:1–5? What did Jesus use to illustrate His answer?

What two things must you do to enter the kingdom of heaven?

Look up *converted* in Strong's Concordance (#G4762). Also read Colossians 3:9–12; 2 Corinthians 5:17; Ephesians 4:22–24.

Look up *humility* in a bible dictionary.

What types of people receive Jesus?

Look up *offense* (offence) in Strong's Concordance (#G4624) and a bible dictionary.

What did Jesus say would be *better to happen* to those who offend one of the little ones?

67

Warning Against Offenses

Matthew 18:1–10

What warning does Jesus give in Matthew 18:7?

What should you do if your hand, foot, or eye offends you? What is it better to have?

Jesus says not to despise the little ones. What does it mean to despise someone? Look up *despise* in Strong's Concordance (#G2706).

Why did Jesus say we should not despise the little ones?

68

Parable of the Lost Sheep

Matthew 18:11–14 and Luke 15:1–7

Why did the Pharisees and scribes murmur against Jesus (Luke 15:1–7)?

In the parable Jesus shared, how many sheep did the man have? How many went astray?

Where did the man go to find the sheep that went astray?

How did the man respond when he found the sheep?

Who are the sheep compared to? What would be the response in heaven?

What is not the will of your Father in heaven (Matthew 18:14)?

69

Forgiving Others

Matthew 18:15–17, 21–35,
and Luke 17:3–4

What is a trespass? Look up *trespass* in Strong's Concordance (#G264).

If someone sins against you, what is the first thing you should do (Matthew 18:15; Luke 17:3)?

Look up *rebuke* in Strong's Concordance (#G2008) and a bible dictionary. Read Galatians 6:1–2 as well.

What would happen if he or she receives your message (Matthew 18:15)? What if he or she does not receive your message?

What is the last resort for seeking a resolution? What would happen if he or she refuses to listen?

What is a *heathen* and *publican*? Look up each word in a bible dictionary.

70

Forgiving Others

Matthew 18:15–17, 21–35,
and Luke 17:3–4

If someone sins against you and he or she asks for forgiveness, should you forgive him or her (Matthew 18:21; Luke 17:3–4)?

Should you put a limit on how many times you forgive someone (Luke 17:4)?

Describe the parable Jesus shares about the kingdom of heaven (Matthew 18:23–35).

71

Rich Young Ruler

Matthew 19:16–26, Mark 10:17–27,
and Luke 18:18–27

What did the man ask Jesus? What was Jesus' initial response?

The man says he has lived by the commandments from his youth and asks if there is anything he lacks. What three things does Jesus say he needs to do in order to be perfect?

How did the young man respond? Why?

What did Jesus say about rich men entering the kingdom of heaven? What did He compare it to?

What did Jesus' disciples ask Him (Matthew 19:25)?

How did Jesus respond to His disciples?

72

Parable of the Vineyard Workers

Matthew 20:1–16

What did Jesus compare the kingdom of heaven to?

What did the householder do?

Explain what the householder did at the first, third, sixth, ninth, and eleventh hour?

What occurred at the twelfth (even) hour? Who received their wages (hire) first?

Why did those hired first murmur against the goodman of the house? How did the goodman of the house respond (Matthew 20:13–15)?

How were the last first and the first last (Matthew 20:16)?

73

Authority and Servanthood

Matthew 20:20–28 and Mark 10:35–45

Besides being the sons of Zebedee, who were the two men (Matthew 10:1–4)? What did their mother ask Jesus?

The sons of Zebedee stated they would be able to drink of the cup Jesus drinks and be baptized with the same baptism. Jesus concurred. In what ways would this happen (Acts 12:1–5; 2 Corinthians 11:23–27; Philippians 4:12; Revelation 1:1–11)?

Who decides the places of those on the left and right of Jesus in His kingdom?

How did the ten disciples respond?

Read Matthew 20:25–26. Based on Jesus' and the ten disciples' response, what was the intent of James' and John's request?

Are disciples to exercise authority over others? If not, why?

Whose behavior are they not to take after? What are they to do (Mark 10:43–44)?

How was Jesus an example to His disciples (Matthew 20:28; Mark 10:45)?

74

Asking in Prayer

Matthew 21:17–22 and Mark 11:20–26

In what condition did Jesus find the fig tree? What did He do next?

Why did the disciples marvel?

Are the disciples able to do the same to the fig tree? How?

What other things will they be able to accomplish? What is the *necessary* condition?

75

Entering the Kingdom

Matthew 21:23–32

What did the chief priests and the elders of the people ask Jesus while He was teaching in the temple? What was Jesus' response?

Why did the chief priests and the elders of the people reason within themselves?

Why did Jesus not answer their initial question?

Jesus did not answer their initial question, but posed one of His own. What did He ask? What was their response?

Look up *harlot* in a bible dictionary.

Why will the publicans and harlots enter the kingdom of God before the chief priests and elders of the people?

76

Parable of the Landowner

Matthew 21:33–46, Mark 12:1–12, and Luke 20:9–19

What did the householder do before going into a far country?

Look up *husbandman* in Strong's Concordance (#G1092).

What did the husbandmen do when the householder sought to receive the fruits from the vineyard?

Why did the householder send his son? What did they do to him? Why?

What will the householder do to the husbandmen when he returns?

Who is the stone that has become the head of the corner (cornerstone) (Acts 4:1–12; Ephesians 2:11–22)?

What will the householder do with the kingdom of God (Matthew 21:43; Acts 10:1–11;18; Colossians 1:25–29)?

Why will those who fall on the stone be broken and those the stone falls on be ground to powder (Isaiah 8:14–15; 1 Peter 2:1–12)?

Why did the chief priests, scribes, and Pharisees seek to lay hands on Jesus? Why were they unable to do it?

77

Parable of the Wedding Feast

Matthew 22:1–14

What did the king do to prepare for the wedding?

What happened when the king sent his servants to invite the people to the wedding?

When the king learned all that had been done, how did he react?

When the invitees were proved unworthy of attending the wedding, how was the wedding furnished with guests? What type of people did he invite (Matthew 22:9–10)?

When the king arrived at the wedding and found a man without a wedding garment, what became of him?

Who will be able to attend the wedding feast (Matthew 22:11–12; Revelation 19:1–9)?

What will happen to those without a wedding garment?

Read a bible commentary on Matthew 22:1–14.

78

The Greatest Commandment

Matthew 22:34–40 and Mark 12:28–31

Who approached Jesus with a question? What was the question? Why was the question asked?

What is the great commandment in the law?

What is the second great commandment in the law?

What else did Jesus say about the great commandments in the law?

Are there any greater commandments than the two Jesus described?

79

Warning Against
Scribes and Pharisees

Matthew 23, Mark 12:38–40,
Luke 11:37–52, and Luke 20:46–47

Where do the scribes and Pharisees sit? What was that place considered to be (Exodus 18:13)? Read Exodus 18 for context.

Considering the scribes and Pharisees, what things did Jesus say they should/should not do? Why (Matthew 23:3–6)?

What are phylacteries? Look up *phylacteries* and *tefillin* in a bible dictionary or encyclopedia. Review Numbers 15:37–41 for information on the borders of garments.

80

Warning Against Scribes and Pharisees

Matthew 23, Mark 12:38–40,
Luke 11:37–52, and Luke 20:46–47

What three things are people not to be called (Matthew 23:8–10)?

What should they be (Matthew 23:11)? Why (Matthew 23:12)?

Jesus gave eight *woe* statements. What did He call the scribes and Pharisees throughout these statements (Matthew 23:13–36)? Describe each statement made against them and what Jesus said they should have done in each statement (if applicable).

81

The Coming of Jesus, the Kingdom of God, and the Age to Come

*Matthew 24:1–25, Mark 13:1–23,
Luke 17:20–37, and Luke 21:5–24*

What did Jesus say about the buildings of the temple?

What did the disciples ask Jesus privately?

What will be considered the beginning of sorrows?

What things must happen before the end will come? What will occur next?

What warnings did Jesus give?

What types of people will show great signs and wonders?

82

The Coming of Jesus, the Kingdom of God, and the Age to Come

*Matthew 24:26–35, Mark 13:24–31,
and Luke 21:25–33*

How fast will the coming of Jesus be (Matthew 24:27)?

What will happen before the appearing of the sign of the Son of man (Matthew 24:29–30)?

How will the Son of man appear?

What will His angels accomplish at His appearing?

What will not pass away?

83

The Coming of Jesus, the Kingdom of God, and the Age to Come

*Matthew 24:36–51, Mark 13:32–37,
Luke 12:35–48, and Luke 21:34–38*

Who knows when Jesus will return (Mark 13:32)?

What warnings does Jesus give concerning His return?

Who are the blessed, faithful, and wise servants?

What will occur upon Jesus' return?

What will happen to those who do not prepare themselves for His coming or are unfaithful in their work?

Look up *watch* in Strong's Concordance (#G1127).

84

Parable of the Ten Virgins
Matthew 25:1–13

Why were the virgins waiting?

Why were some wise and some foolish (Matthew 25:3–4)?

What were the virgins doing while waiting for the bridegroom to arrive?

Who is the bridegroom?

When the bridegroom arrived, which of the ten virgins were prepared to meet him right away?

What did the foolish virgins ask the wise? What was their response?

Who was allowed to enter the marriage (Matthew 25:10)?

The other virgins came to enter the marriage as well. When did they arrive? What was the Lord's response to them?

85

Parable of the Talents

Matthew 25:14–30 and Luke 19:11–27

Why did Jesus speak this parable (Luke 19:11)?

What was the nobleman's purpose (Luke 19:12)?

What did the nobleman give the people of the far country in Matthew? Luke?

In Luke, what did the nobleman say to the people? How did the people respond (Luke 19:14)?

What occurred when the nobleman returned (Matthew 25:19; Luke 19:15)? Outline what the first two servants brought him.

What did the first two servants receive in return?

What did the third servant do with what he received?

How did the servant feel about the nobleman? What did the servant say about him?

What did the nobleman say about the type of servant he was (Matthew 25:26; Luke 19:22)?

What did the nobleman do with what he gave to the third servant? Why?

What happened to the third servant in Matthew and Luke?

86

Gathering of the Sheep and Goats

Matthew 25:31–46

Who will be brought to Jesus when He comes in His glory and all the angels with Him? How will they be divided?

Who is the King? How long had the kingdom been prepared for the people?

Why did the people on the right inherit the kingdom (Matthew 25:35–40)?

What did the King say to those on His left hand?

Where will they go? Who was that place prepared for?

Why did the people on the left *inherit* their punishment (Matthew 25:42–45)?

After the King speaks to those on the left and right, where will each group go?

87

Parable of the Growing Seed

Mark 4:26–29

Read Mark 4:1–20 for context.

What is the kingdom of God compared to?

How does the seed spring up and grow? What does the man do in the meantime?

Who brings forth fruit of herself? How?

How does the man know when the harvest has come? What does he do?

Look up *sickle* in a bible dictionary.

What will occur when the harvest of the earth is ripe (Revelation 14:14–20)? Read Revelation 14 for context.

88

Those Among Us

Mark 9:33–41 and Luke 9:46–50

Why were the disciples disputing among themselves?

What two things did Jesus say in response (Mark 9:35–37)?

When Jesus finished speaking, what did John say he and the disciples witnessed (Mark 9:38; Luke 9:49)?

Why did the disciples forbid someone from casting out devils in Jesus' name?

What three things did Jesus say in response (Mark 9:39–41)?

89

The Body and Blood of Jesus

Matthew 26:17–30, Mark 14:12–26,
and Luke 22:7–30

Look up *Passover* in a bible dictionary.

While eating with His disciples, Jesus presented bread before them. What did He do with the bread? What is the bread (Matthew 26:26; Mark 14:22; Luke 22:19)?

Jesus also took a cup and presented it before them. What is the fruit of the vine (Matthew 26:27–28; Mark 14:23–24; Luke 22:20)? Who and what is Jesus' blood shed for?

When will be the next time Jesus drinks of the fruit of the vine (Matthew 26:29; Mark 14:25; Luke 22:15–16)?

Look up *Lord's Supper* in a bible dictionary.

90

Who is My Neighbor?

Luke 10:25–37

Describe the conversation between Jesus and the lawyer.

What happened to the man traveling to Jericho?

What did the first, second, and third person do when they saw the man?

Look up *priest*, *Levite*, and *Samaritan* in a bible dictionary.

What is the significance of the help of the Samaritan over the other two people?

What did Jesus then ask the lawyer? How did the lawyer respond?

Who is the lawyer's neighbor?

91

Watch What You Say and Do

Luke 12:1–12

What is the leaven of the Pharisees? Read Luke 11 for context.

What things will be revealed, known, heard in the light, and proclaimed upon the housetops?

Who are we to fear? Who are we not to fear? Why (Luke 12:4–7)?

What will happen if we confess Jesus before men? What will happen if we do not?

What will happen to those who speak a word against the Son of man? Blasphemy against the Holy Spirit?

Who will teach us what to say if we are brought before church authorities and people of prestige and power?

92

Being Rich Toward God

Luke 12:13–34

What did someone in Jesus' company say to Him?

What was Jesus' response to the man? What was His response to the group?

Does a person's life consist of the abundance of things he or she possesses?

Jesus spoke a parable about a rich man. What did the rich man do?

What did the rich man say to his soul?

Why did God call the rich man a fool?

What types of people are not rich toward God (Luke 12:21)?

How can a person be rich toward God (Matthew 6:19–21; Luke 12:32–34)?

93

Waiting for the Repentant Souls

Luke 13:1–9

What did Jesus say after hearing about the Galilaeans (Luke 13:1–5)?

Were the people worse sinners because of how they died? What was Jesus' point (Luke 13:3, Luke 13:5)?

Jesus told a parable about a man. What did he do? What did he look for?

How long did the man wait seeking fruit? What did he tell his dresser of the vineyard he wanted to do?

What did the dresser of the vineyard say to his lord and what did he desire to do (Luke 13:8–9)?

Considering Luke 13:3 and Luke 13:5, what was the purpose of the parable (2 Peter 3:9)?

94

Places of Honor

Luke 14:1–11

Why did Jesus speak a parable to the group (Luke 14:7)?

When being invited to a wedding (or any place) without assigned seating, where should you sit? Why?

What does the parable illustrate (Luke 14:11)?

95
Parable of the Banquet Invitees

Luke 14:12–24

Why was the man not to invite his brothers, kinsmen, and rich neighbors when he prepares dinner or supper?

What is the reward for following Jesus' guidance?

When one of them with Jesus said, '*blessed is he that shall eat in the kingdom of God*,' what example did Jesus give in response?

When the master of the house sent out invitations to his great supper, what responses did he receive?

What did the master of the house do after hearing the servant's message?

How was the master's house filled? What will happen to those who were originally invited?

96

Parable of the Lost Coin

Luke 15:8–10
(review Luke 15:1–10 for context)

When the woman with ten pieces of silver loses one, what does she do?

How did she search for the coin?

What did the woman do once she found the missing coin?

What does the parable illustrate (Luke 15:10)?

How many angels are there (Daniel 7:9–10; Hebrews 12:22–24; Revelation 5:11–12)?

97

Parable of the Two Sons

Luke 15:11–32

What did the younger son desire from his father?

What did the younger son do with the substance he received?

What happened to the younger son after he spent all he had and a famine came upon the land?

What happened when he came to himself? What did he decide to say to his father?

What did the father do when he saw his younger son a great way off? How did the father respond to what the younger son said in his return?

How did the elder son respond to his brother's return?

What did the father say to the elder son in response?

What was there to be merry about?

98

Parable of the Unjust Steward

Luke 16:1–12

What did the rich man accuse his steward of doing?

What did the steward say to himself? What was he unwilling and ashamed to do?

What did the steward do in order to prepare for his future (being put out of the stewardship)?

Why did the lord commend the steward for what he did in Luke 16:4–7?

Look up *mammon* in Strong's Concordance (#G3126).

Why were the disciples to make to themselves friends of the mammon of unrighteousness (Luke 16:9)? What will they receive when they fail?

What does Jesus say about the faithful and unjust (Luke 16:10)?

Explain the two statements Jesus gives about not being faithful in Luke 16:11–12.

99

Parable of the Rich Man and Lazarus

Luke 16:19–31

How did the rich man live? Look up *sumptuously* in Strong's Concordance (#G2988).

Describe Lazarus and his life.

When each man died, where did they go and how were they treated?

The rich man called out to Abraham. What two things did he ask of him (Luke 16:24)? What did Abraham say in response?

What was the rich man's next request? Why (Luke 16:27–28)?

Why did the rich man want someone from the dead to go to his father's house? Why did Abraham deny his request?

100

A Duty to Forgive

Luke 17:5–10

Why did the apostles say to the Lord, '*increase our faith?*' What issue was Jesus speaking on (Luke 17:3–4)?

What size faith did Jesus say could uproot a sycamine tree?

Look up *sycamine tree* in a bible dictionary or encyclopedia (ensure the definition/description speaks of the tree's characteristics).

Jesus gives an example concerning a servant (Luke 17:7–9). What was Jesus' point (Luke 17:10)?

101

Parable of the Two Praying Men

Luke 18:9–14

Why did Jesus speak this parable?

What two men entered the temple?

What did the Pharisee say in his prayer?

Describe the publican and his prayer to God.

Which of the two men were justified before God? Why?

Look up *justified* in Strong's Concordance (#G1344).

102

Light and Darkness
John 3:16–21

Who was Jesus speaking to (John 3:1–2)?

How does God feel about the world? What did God do?

How can someone perish? How can someone have eternal life?

Why did God send His Son into the world (John 3:17)?

How can the world be saved?

Who are those that are condemned?

What was the condemnation (John 3:19)? Look up *condemnation* in Strong's Concordance (#G2920).

The light has come into the world. Who is the light (John 1:1–14)?

God loved the world. What did men love? Why (John 3:19–20)?

Who are those that come into the light? Why?

103

The Father and Son

John 5:19–30 (review John 5)

What things can the Son do?

Who should men honor?

How can men receive eternal life (John 5:24)?

Summarize John 5:24–30.

Why are Jesus' judgments just (John 5:30)?

104

Bread of Life

John 6:22–71 (review John 6)

Why were the people seeking Jesus in John 6:26?

What did Jesus say the people should labor for?

What is the meat that endures unto everlasting life?

How can a person never hunger or thirst (John 6:35)?

How can a person have everlasting life (John 6:40, John 6:47, John 6:54, John 6:58)?

How did Jesus compare the bread of their fathers and the bread of life (John 6:48–51)?

Jesus spoke of eating His flesh and drinking His blood in John 6:53–58. What was He referring to? What did it mean (John 6:35)?

Who can come to the Father (John 6:65)?

105

Jesus' Teaching

John 7:14–18 (review John 7:1–18)

What were the people at the feast in Judea saying about Jesus (John 7:12)? What did they say as He taught in the temple (John 7:14–15)?

Where did Jesus' doctrine (teaching) come from?

How can you know if someone's doctrine is of God or from him or herself (John 7:17)?

When people speak of themselves, what are they after (John 7:18)?

As told in John 7:18, how can no unrighteousness be within a person?

106

The Good Shepherd

John 10:1–18

Who are thieves and robbers (John 10:1)?

Who is the shepherd of the sheep (Matthew 26:31–32; John 10:13; Hebrews 13:20–21)?

Look up *porter* in Strong's Concordance (#G2377).

How do the sheep know where to go (John 10:3–4, John 10:14)?

Why will sheep not follow strangers? What will they do if they meet a stranger?

Who is the door of the sheep? How are the sheep saved?

Why did the thief come? Why did Jesus come (John 10:10)?

Who are hirelings? Do they care about the sheep?

What happens when hirelings see wolves coming? What happens to the sheep?

Are there other sheep (John 10:16)? Where are they (Acts 10–11; Ephesians 2:10–22)?

How many folds will there be? How many shepherds? Read Ephesians 4:1–6.

107

Sheep in the Father's Hand

John 10:19–30

Why was there a division among the Jews (John 10:19–21)?

What did the Jews ask Jesus? What was Jesus' response (John 10:24–25)?

What bears witness of Jesus?

Why were the Jews who were around Jesus not one of His sheep (John 10:26)?

What six things does Jesus say about His sheep (John 10:27–28)?

Who gave Jesus His sheep? How does Jesus describe His Father?

108

The Hour of Glorification

John 12:20–43

What did the Greeks attending the feast desire?

What did Jesus say in response (John 12:23)?

Describe the statement Jesus made about the corn of wheat and compare it to Jesus' life. How would Jesus' death bring forth much fruit (John 3:16–17; Romans 5; 1 Peter 3:18–22)?

What will happen to those who love (and hate) their lives?

How can a person be where Jesus is (John 12:26)?

109

The Hour of Glorification

John 12:20–43

Why was Jesus' soul troubled (Matthew 26:36–46)?

What did Jesus say to His Father (John 12:28)? What was His Father's response (John 12:28)? Why (John 12:29–30)?

What will happen to the prince of this world (John 12:31)? Who is he (2 Corinthians 4:1–4; Ephesians 2:2)?

How will all men be drawn unto Jesus (John 12:32)? What did this signify (John 12:33, John 18:28–19:16)?

What did the people hear about the Christ in the law (Psalm 89:36–37, Psalm 110:1–4; Isaiah 9:6–7, Isaiah 53)?

What did Jesus say concerning light and darkness (see John 3:18–21, John 8:12, John 12:46 as well)?

Why did some believe and some not believe (John 12:37–43)? Who were those that believed (John 12:42–43)? Did they confess Him openly? Why or why not?

110

Servanthood and Love

John 13

What did Jesus do after He knew that the Father had given all things into His hands (John 13:5–6)?

Why did Jesus wash His disciples' feet (John 13:15)?

What did Jesus say in John 13:16?

How did Jesus say the disciples could be happy (John 13:17)?

Describe the events in John 13:18–33.

What is the new commandment Jesus gave (John 13:34)? Why (John 13:35)?

111

The Way Home

John 14:1–31

Summarize John 14:1–4.

What did Jesus say in response to Thomas' question (John 14:6–7)?

What did Jesus say in response to Phillip's question (John 14:9–14)?

If the disciples loved Jesus, what would they do (John 14:15)? What would Jesus do in response?

Who is the Comforter and what will He do (John 14:16–18, John 14:26, John 15:26–27)?

What did Jesus say in response to Judas' (not Iscariot's) question (John 14:23–31)?

112

The Arrival of the Comforter

John 16:5–14

When will the Comforter come (John 16:7)?

Look up *reprove* in Strong's Concordance (#G1651).

When the Comforter comes, what three things will He reprove the world of? Review the following scriptures for the first (John 15:18–25); second (Acts 3:1–16); and third (John 12:31; Acts 26:1–18; Colossians 2:13–15; Hebrews 2:14; 1 John 3:8).

What is the Comforter also known as (John 16:13)?

List what Jesus says the Spirit of Truth will accomplish (John 16:13–14).

113

The True Vine
and the Branches
John 15:1–17

Who is the true vine? Who is the husbandman?

What will the husbandman do (John 15:2)? Why?

How were the disciples made clean (John 15:3)?

Jesus speaks about abiding in Him (John. 15:4–10). List each statement Jesus gives concerning abiding in Him and the result.

Can fruit bear of itself? Why or why not (John 15:4–5)?

How is the Father glorified (John 15:8)?

What is Jesus' commandment (John 15:12, 17)?

Why does Jesus call the disciples His friends (John 15:13–15)?

Why did Jesus choose and ordain the disciples (John 7:16)?

Look up *ordain* in a bible dictionary or encyclopedia.

114

The Great Commission

Matthew 28:16–20

Read Matthew 26:36–28:20. Describe the events in Matthew 28 leading to His appearance to the 11 disciples in Galilee.

What did Jesus do when the 11 disciples went to the mountain in Galilee (Matthew 28:16)?

What was given to Jesus (Matthew 28:18)?

List the commands Jesus gave to the disciples.

How did Jesus comfort His disciples (Matthew 28:20)?

115

Reflection

Share your thoughts and experiences while studying *Living for the Kingdom: Teaching What Jesus Taught*.

What decisions have you made as a disciple since completing *Living for the Kingdom: Teaching What Jesus Taught*?

In what ways can you fulfill the Great Commission in your home, local church, and community (to include online)?

Read the book of Acts to learn how Jesus' commission was realized after His ascension into heaven.

I pray *Living for the Kingdom: Teaching What Jesus Taught* has been a great blessing to you and your development as a disciple of Jesus. Please internalize what you have learned and share them with your friends, family members, and fellow disciples. Impress upon them the importance of learning and obeying Jesus' commands, as it is His commission to all believers. Continue to build upon your studies and return to this book as a resource.

LESSON LISTING
WITH SCRIPTURES

SCRIPTURE LISTING
WITH LESSONS

Scripture	Lesson #	Lesson Title
MATTHEW		
Matthew 5:1–12	5	Beatitudes
Matthew 5:4–5	6	Beatitudes
Matthew 5:6–7	7	Beatitudes
Matthew 5:8–12	8	Beatitudes
Matthew 5:13	9	Salt
Matthew 5:14–16	10	Light
Matthew 5:17–20	13–14	Law and Commandments
Matthew 5:21–26	15–16	Anger and Conflict
Matthew 5:27–32	17	Adultery and Lust
Matthew 5:31–32	18–19	Marriage and Divorce
Matthew 5:33–37	20	Oaths and Vows
Matthew 5:38–42	21	Give and Take
Matthew 5:43–48	22	Love and Mercy
Matthew 6:1–4	23	Giving
Matthew 6:5–13	24–27	Prayer
Matthew 6:14–15	28–30	Forgiveness

(com)mission™
PUBLISHING

www.commissionpubs.com
info@commissionpubs.com

www.ingramcontent.com/pod-product-compliance
Lightning Source LLC
Chambersburg PA
CBHW070807050426
42452CB00011B/1927